AdviseHERy

Board

Karen Colligan, Lynn Forbes,
and Jackie Kleinman

www.adviseheryboard.com

ISBN: 978-0-692-06606-5

To our moms, Thelma, Kathleen, and Rose,
our original personal board of directors.
We are who we are because of you.

TABLE OF CONTENTS

PREFACE

This book is for women who want to move their businesses to the next level, are thinking about starting a business, or have a specific work issue to solve. It was written by Karen, Jackie, and Lynn, three smart and sassy entrepreneurs with varied skills and professional backgrounds who developed a unique system for gaining significant business clarity and growth. They call it the AdviseHERy Board, and it's their custom-designed board of directors—and a whole lot more. Each had her own reasons for needing an AdviseHERy Board.

Karen

I was sick to death of corporate America. The Jersey girl in me knew I had to do it my way. In 2000 I started PeopleThink, an organizational development company, delivering my secret sauce to big and small companies. Quite frankly, I was exhausted from trying to figure it all out on my own. Where, oh where, could I find people who would tell it to me straight and help me stretch my thinking? Lynn and Jackie stretched me like a rubber band.

Lynn

I was a newbie entrepreneur when Jackie, Karen, and I decided to start the AdviseHERy Board. I had a boatload of corporate experience in traditional and digital media as a journalist, editor, and content development expert, but I knew next to zilch about running my own business. It was scary. Would I be successful? Would I ever make a decent living again? I had a lot to learn. Turns out, I was in great company.

Jackie

In my first life, my twenties, I was the best, most fun dental hygienist in San Francisco. When I realized I needed something more than "brush, floss, rinse, repeat" in my life, I went back to school, did a spin in corporate America, and decided I wanted to be on my own. I opened my financial planning practice, KB Financial Advisors, in 2002. I worked hard, gathering ideal clients and growing a successful practice. I knew my leadership style needed fine-tuning. Thank goodness, Lynn and Karen helped me see the light.

Here's our story...

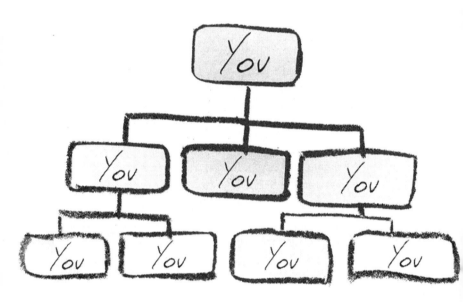

INTRODUCTION

The AdvisHERy Board

Stalled, stunted, and stuck, Karen was searching for a way to take her business to the next level. She decided to gather trusted, smart, entrepreneurial women to help her. She invited Lynn and Jackie to her dining room table, pulled out a bag of magic markers, set up a flip chart, and *voila!* the AdviseHERy Board was born.

We had no idea this venture would be one of the most dynamic business and personal experiences of our lives. It turned out that we were just the right mix of people at just the right time, in just the right place for the concept to blossom. Karen wanted to expand her organizational development company; Jackie's financial services firm was flourishing, and yet she needed a kick in the pants; Lynn had left the corporate world to start her own business and was feeling unsettled about it.

Collectively, our wisdom, expertise, and shared values created the perfect environment for business ideas to flourish. The AdviseHERy Board became our safe haven to talk shop, dream big, catch each other when we trip, and hold our feet to the fire when the going got tough.

You know the entrepreneurial life. You're the sales team, the finance department, the admin, and the IT team. There are no off-sites. The computer and phone are your only connections to the outside world. There's no paid vacation, matching 401(k), or sick leave. Not only does the buck stop here, but you are the buck. Most important, you don't have a reliable way to test your ideas and run new projects up the flagpole. You're on your own, sistah, and it's lonely out here.

Or so it seems. According to the National Women's Business Council, *in 2015, there were 10 million women-owned businesses, compared to 7.8 million in 2007.* Women are jumping into the entrepreneurial circle and designing their own futures by creating the work that's right for them. And for many women, the initial excitement of starting their own businesses is quickly overshadowed by the reality of what it takes to make a business successful. The three reasons women-owned businesses fail are a lack of confidence, capability, and capital.*

---

* Cherie Blair, "Empowering Women, Driving Growth," Foundation for Women, www.cherieblairfoundation.org.

Clearly, we need all the help we can get.

Like most businesswomen, we sought help and support by joining professional groups, attending association meetings and online forums, and going to conferences. We picked up some good ideas and met some interesting people, but we realized we needed more individualized attention. We're guessing that you do too.

AdviseHERy Board to the rescue!

We are an executive board/ Girl Scout troop/ mastermind group rolled into one

We leave our egos at the door

We laugh a lot

We genuinely listen to each other

We say the stuff no one else will tell us

We've got each other's backs

We're tough and kind

We are full-time business coaches and part-time shrinks

We are strong and opinionated, and we speak our minds

We show up and are always prepared

We trust and respect each other

We bring both our successes and failures to the table

We come up with solutions to tough business issues

If you do it right, your AdviseHERy Board will become an important component in your success arsenal for building your business. Here is why it works for us.

We're confidantes. We are positive and proactive—no whining allowed. (However, there may be wine-ing after the meeting.) We have created a methodology that has proven to be reliable, effective, and just plain fun. That is what this book is all about. Take our quiz on the next page to assess your AdviseHERy Board readiness. We have work to do, so let's get going!

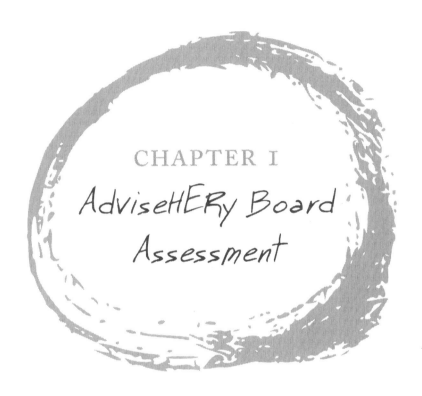

CHAPTER I

AdviseHERy Board
Assessment

Check all that apply:

☐ Your friends are so sick of listening to you whine about your business that they've stopped answering your phone calls

☐ Your client base isn't growing, and you don't like the clients you do have

☐ You have the same goals year after year— and let's be honest, even you don't believe you can achieve them

☐ You go to the grocery store for human contact

☐ Your bank account is as lonely as you are

☐ Your Law of Attraction is turning into Murphy's Law

☐ You're so involved in the nitty-gritty of running your business that you forget why you started the business in the first place

☐ You pick up the phone to make a sales call and end up calling your mother

☐ Your last vacation was...wait, when was that?

☐ You know there's *juuussst* something missing

How did you do? Do more than two scenarios strike a chord? Are you ready to turn those cringe-worthy feelings into action? Keep reading; we'll show you how.

CHAPTER 2

Forming Your
AdviseHERy Board

All groups need a head honcho, someone who has the vision and tenacity to make an idea a reality. For us, that person was Karen. Here is her story.

I was tired of being in my own head. I needed new ideas and fresh energy. I started with the essentials: What was my purpose, and what were my outcomes? My purpose was clear. I wanted to surround myself with people who could help me focus and think differently. My outcomes were to position my business for continued growth and to build an exit strategy.

The trick was to find the right people. With my organizational development background, I had a leg up on how to intelligently make the right choices, yet it was still a crapshoot. I searched my contact list for women who would benefit from the model and wanted to build thriving businesses.

Great things do not just happen by impulse but as a succession of small things linked together.

— *Vincent Van Gogh* —

It was important to me to find people with similar values so we could build a culture of trust. These women needed to be kick-ass smart and not afraid to push each other to think differently and stretch boundaries. I wanted to surround myself with women who would work hard, laugh often and hold each other accountable in a kind-spirited way. And in keeping with my New Jersey roots, I felt that a little bit of irreverence was a must. Eagerness to challenge the status quo, curiosity, and a huge heart were non-negotiables. Wallflowers need not apply.

With clarity accomplished, my choices were obvious. Lynn and Jackie, look out! I was comin' after you, and I was not going to take no for an answer.

> The person who says it cannot be done should not interrupt the person who is doing it.
>
> — *Chinese proverb* —

This was not going to be another gabfest. It was going to be a serious work group, focused on helping members propel their businesses forward. I had known both Lynn and Jackie for many years, but they didn't know each other. They were in completely different industries and lived in different parts of the Bay Area. This was where my gut came into play. Based on our different skill sets, I knew I had the right ingredients in hand.

I chose Jackie because she is a financial wiz and can look at our businesses from a numbers perspective. She had been self-employed for fifteen years and had successfully built her business to the stage where she was taking on partners. Jackie wanted to create an exit strategy, albeit not for several years, with the certainty of leaving a legacy.

Lynn comes from the media and digital world and has more technical chops; she keeps us current. She has strong writing, editing, and marketing expertise. Lynn also has startup experience, so she is very resourceful. She's a big-picture thinker and gets us out of our heads. Every time she opens her mouth, another idea comes out.

I had previous experience with an advisory board. My business is financially stable, and I plan to grow and position it in order to ultimately sell it. My specific experience in leadership and team development, along with being a seasoned facilitator, is invaluable. I am extremely organized and am the unofficial archivist, note taker, and keeper of records. I keep the team on track and the band playing.

I reached out to Jackie and Lynn and explained my idea for an advisory board. We scheduled an initial meeting and decided it was a great idea, and the journey began.

We were not the lean, mean, fighting machine we are today right out of the gate. It took time for us to gel and to find our rhythm, to feel safe to express our dreams and vulnerabilities. It was a process. In essence, you are creating a new team, and you need to have a discussion about what that means for your AdviseHERy Board. Most of us have been on an ugly team where there is a lack of communication, egos galore, values that don't map, undefined roles, and fuzzy goals. Though it's hard to describe, you probably also know what it's like to be on one of those special, high-performing teams. You just know when you're a part of one.

How To SELECT Your AdviseHERy Board Members

Determine the desired size of your team. We recommend no more than three to five people. If your group is too big, you will not be able to give each other the time and undivided attention necessary to have strong, meaningful conversations and brainstorming sessions. Our magic number is three.

Look for diverse skills, expertise, and industries. The diversity of talent is important. You want people who will push you to think differently and look at an issue from multiple perspectives. If you want to invite only those who think like you, don't bother forming the group.

Similar values are essential. We cannot stress this enough. If you do not see eye to eye on such things as integrity, work ethic, empathy, and humor, it ain't gonna work.

Bring in strong leaders who will be problem solvers and innovative thinkers. Seek out people who have a positive, can-do attitude.

Only invite members who are committed to the idea and are willing to dedicate one year to give the group a chance to get it right.

Include someone who is structured and willing to be the hard-ass to keep the group on point.

Oh, did we say this is a serious commitment? Everyone must pinky-swear that she will work to make the AdviseHERy Board a success.

The most important thing is to create an AdviseHERy Board that fits your specific needs. Be bold and creative.

For more ideas about how to form a great team, read The Wisdom of Teams by Jon R. Katzenbach and Douglas K. Smith. It's packed with words of wisdom about highly functioning teams, such as "Teams outperform individuals acting alone, especially when performance requires multiple skills, judgments and experience."

Okay, you've selected your board members. Now what? Your first decisions as a group are to identify your AdviseHERy Board's purpose and outcomes, rules of engagement, and meeting structure.

PURPOSE AND OUTCOMES

This is where your group comes together to focus on the why of your AdviseHERy Board the ultimate reason to create the board and stay together. Each individual in your group must proclaim her purpose and desired outcomes. In our case, we each wanted something very specific related to our businesses. Karen wanted to build an exit strategy for PeopleThink—a plan to build the business so it could be sold down the road. Jackie wanted to look at how to work on the business and not so much in the business; she also wanted to create additional services. Lynn wanted to build the infrastructure for her business, examining the mechanics: how it would operate, who would participate, and how to build multiple revenue streams.

Why do you want to create an AdviseHERy Board? Write it down! Is your business stuck, and you're scared out of your mind? Do you feel isolated and tired of talking to yourself out loud? Have you reached a plateau and need help getting to the next level? Maybe everything is humming along, and you simply want a sounding board.

Whatever your purpose, get clear about realistic goals. Do you want to increase your revenue by a certain percent in one year? Feel secure about hiring staff? Sell your business? Create a succession plan and start living that retirement dream in five years? The AdviseHERy Board process works far better if you know very specifically what you want out of it.

What we have discovered through our journey is that our purposes and outcomes will shift. As life happens, it is important to pay attention to your business to determine whether there are other ideas to incorporate, trends to consider, or modifications to be made. Being focused and flexible is key. You must always be looking down the road and striving for your goals. However, don't be so rigid that you miss an opportunity along the way.

RULES OF ENGAGEMENT

How will you play together in the sandbox? Defining the rules of engagement will help you focus on how you want to operate as a group and what is important in order to thrive. Don't get hung up on this part; use common sense. Good rules equal good results: start and end meetings on time, establish roles for the facilitator and participants, turn off cell phones when the meeting starts, be accountable to do what you say you are going to do, and commit to confidentiality.

As we practiced our rules of engagement, communication principles evolved. We have learned how to gently push each other to expand our thinking; we are never degrading, and we never discount an idea or action. Confidentiality is crucial, and we provide feedback in a kind-spirited manner that will enhance the conversation; we speak the truth. As your group evolves, your communication principles will evolve with you.

Schedule some time during your first meeting to establish your rules of engagement. You might have three rules, or you might have ten. The number doesn't matter. What matters is your ability to document them and incorporate them into the fabric of your AdviseHERy Board.

> If you really want to do something, you will find a way. If you don't, you will find an excuse.
>
> — *James Rohn* —

CHAPTER 3

Meeting Structure

You're intrigued by our fabulous AdviseHERy Board concept, and you want one of your very own to nourish and grow your business. Let's make that happen.

You've identified your members: people with whom you share similar values in order to build a culture of trust. They are smart, they are committed, and they have good hearts and a great sense of humor. You have figured out your purpose and outcomes. Now get a date on the calendar for your first meeting.

It's showtime! Get those magic markers out and make your AdviseHERy Board real. Final decisions need to be made about meeting structure, agenda format, and the rules of engagement. Although it may seem tedious, it won't take long, and it's time well spent.

Decide how you will capture your ideas and next steps. We use a brainstorming system called mind mapping, a visual thinking tool that structures information and allows us to better examine, understand, and generate new ideas. Karen uses this tool extensively in her work, but you don't have to be an expert to make it work for you. All you need is a flip chart and a bunch of magic markers in a rainbow of colors. We provide more details on mind mapping in Chapter 5. Whatever you use to collect ideas, be sure it can be archived so you can refer back to the information later.

MEETING LOGISTICS

Without a blueprint, things fall apart, or at least they get messy and unproductive. Without a foundation, the house is not stable. You'll get frustrated and lose heart, and after all the hard work of planning your AdviseHERy Board, that would be a real shame. Keep going! Creating synergy with your members and making real progress on your business goals are straight ahead.

Here are the logistics for your AdviseHERy Board meeting structure. This is your board of directors meeting, so take it seriously.

When

Decide whether you will meet during a work day, in the evening, or on a weekend. We usually meet at 12:30 p.m. on a work day, although the exact day of the week varies. We hold our meetings during the work day because we consider them to be integral to our businesses. If you work for a corporation, the meetings are scheduled during the day, right? Committing to and taking meetings seriously are the keys to success. These meetings are sacred, and canceling is unacceptable.

When will your meetings be held?

How Often

It's important to meet every four to six weeks for consistency and to keep the mojo going. In four years, we have had only one six-week gap between meetings. When we got together that time, we were all in desperate need for an AdviseHERy Board fix. When push comes to shove, we do a conference call or a live video meeting (see Chapter 5 for conferencing ideas).

How often will you meet?

Length

We recommend two to three hours. Your meeting structure and how many people you have on your AdviseHERy Board will dictate the length of your meetings. You decide what is appropriate.

How long will your meetings be?

Where

Our initial plan was to have all of our meetings in person, and to rotate the location so we could take turns hosting and facilitating. Schedules, traffic, and life made that plan too complicated. Now we meet at Jackie's swank office in downtown San Francisco, or if necessary, we meet virtually by phone or GoToMeeting.

Where will your meetings be held?

Facilitator

Changing up who leads each meeting sounds good in theory, but for us things work best when Karen, a black belt in organization, runs the show. She is also the one who takes meeting notes (by hand!) and keeps a file (a paper manila folder!) of all our documents and treasures: meeting notes, next steps, mind maps, inspirational quotes, and our Lumina Spark work style portraits (see Chapter 5). Don't feel sorry for her—she loves it.

Who will be your facilitator?

MEETING AGENDA

Kick-off

We start our time together with food. Jackie always brings in lunch from the Mediterranean place down the street: chicken, eggplant salad, hummus, and pita bread. Yum! We chit-chat and share what's going on in our personal lives. This can include restaurant finds, books, travel and shoes. Sometimes there are even surprise gifts. (Thank you for that aromatherapy spray, Jackie!) You may decide that your AdviseHERy Board is strictly business, and you can draw the line at keeping the discussion professional. That's fine. This is how we do it, but you can create your own reality.

How will you kick off your meetings?

Grounding Exercise

Once the munching is over, we start with a grounding exercise so we can be present, focus on our businesses, and leave the rest of the world behind.

We've started some of our meetings with a deep-thought question such as "What do you want to do this year that has nothing to do with work? If today were your last day on earth, what would you want to be remembered for? What makes you smile?"

Recently we've been reading a quote from a great book called Buddhist Bootcamp by Timber Hawkeye. It is packed with words of wisdom, including our favorite from Albert Einstein: "Everyone is a genius, but if you judge a fish on its ability to climb a tree, it will live its entire life believing it is stupid." For more of our favorite books and resources, see the Recommended Reading section.

What will your grounding exercise be?

ORGANIZING TIME

Check-in

We start with a round-robin session. Each person has five minutes to explain what she needs from the meeting that day. Some examples: discuss a complicated client, receive input on business planning and strategies, talk through a sensitive issue she's having with a colleague, and celebrate a success. From this check-in, we then determine how to appropriately allocate our meeting time. Sometimes one of us may only need a few minutes. Other times, someone may need a lot of help, and we dedicate the majority of the meeting to her. Once you have a handful of meetings under your belt, you'll begin to understand the rhythm and cadence of your group and what to expect from each get-together.

How will you allocate your meeting time?

Heart and Soul of the Meeting

This is the essence of the AdviseHERy Board

meeting, the meat and potatoes. It's the reason you're participating. Business-altering ideas and observations happen right here, right now. Whatever you need, this is when you'll get it.

Each person takes center stage for thirty to forty minutes, beginning with a review of notes and action items from the prior meeting to measure progress. It is the time to talk, listen, and be open to new ideas. Feel confident that this is a safe zone where confidentiality is non-negotiable and trust is established and built. Let 'er rip.

Here's a real-life example. As Jackie's company was growing, she considered going from a sole proprietorship to a limited liability corporation (LLC) and bringing on a partner. Over a number of meetings, we helped Jackie think through the complexity of the decision, analyzing every pro and con we could uncover. The discovery included discussions about roles and responsibilities, how the company culture may be impacted, the financial structure, and how the current client base would be affected. The final answer was that she should do it, and she hasn't looked back.

What business challenges do you need help with?

Wrap-up

Confirm next meeting date, location, and time, as well as any follow-ups. Depending on the hour of the day, bring out the cocktails or cupcakes!

How will you end your meeting?

CHAPTER 4
Communication

Communication can make or break any relationship, whether business or personal, and it is one of the most important keys to the success of your AdviseHERy Board. Our communication structure is rooted in our rules of engagement (Chapter 2), meeting structure (Chapter 3), and tools (Chapter 5). From this structure, other subtle yet powerful techniques to support and guide each other have evolved.

OUR COMMUNICATION STYLE

Tough kindness is the core of our communication style. If something needs to be said, we make the point clear, but never in a demeaning way and always from a place of respect. Here are our favorite ways to get the message across.

1. Complete focus. When each person has the floor, we're all ears.

2. Respectful banter. Even if we don't agree, we let the conversation take its course.

3. Harmless sarcasm. "Oh, sure, puh-lease waste more time on this issue. Oh, and

why don't you pour more money into it while you're at it?" This is accompanied by extreme voice intonations, flailing of hands, and rolling of eyes.

4. Uncovering the truth. We ask a lot of thoughtful, probing questions that often reveal treasures more precious than an archeological dig at Giza.

5. Gentle verbal smackdowns. "You know, is this really worth all the anxiety? Is this taking you off course into the wild blue yonder? Shouldn't you just pick up your big girl panties and make a decision?" You get the idea.

6. Self-deprecation. "This reminds me of the time I spent a whole year tiptoeing around Patricia before I had the guts to find a new assistant. What was I thinking?"

7. Occasional use of the F-bomb to express frustration, dismay, and camaraderie. "Who the f— does he think he's dealing with?"

8. Belly laughs. We laugh a lot. Laughing breaks the tension, moves us from point A to B in a conversation, and is more restorative than a big barrel of awesome.

9. Honoring opinions. We use them as a springboard to introduce other ideas. "I get that you're really torn about accepting that board position. Does being on the board work for you at this point in your business? Will there be an opportunity to accept the position in a year or two, when you have more time?" (True story.)

10. Helpful reminders. When needed, we refer back to the notes from previous meetings. There have been plenty of times when our archivist, Karen, has checked back to see what was said about a particular issue. All she has to do is read the notes out loud for us to realize that an issue has come up over and over again. Oh, the cringing and humiliation! It's time to make a change.

11. Holding up the mirror. "Do you see what we see?"

12. Commiseration. There is nothing more powerful than knowing someone has your back.

OUR SECRET CODE

When Jackie screams out, "She's so blue!" no one blinks an eye. We know exactly what she means. Karen has assessed us in the Lumina Spark personality methodology (Chapter 5) and has trained us how to use the system in our everyday lives. We know that when Jackie yells, "Blue!" she's referring to someone who is a creature of detail and who needs more evidence in order to make a decision.

Lumina Spark lingo is just one of the many secret codes and verbal shortcuts we have developed in our years together. For instance, "I looovvvve that idea" means "I support your thinking, but I'm not crazy about what just came out of your mouth." Also, "Let me go get you a hot cup of crybaby soup" means "Stop your whining already." "Next!" means "This part of the conversation is played out. Let's move it, people. There's nothing to see here." We often say, "Shall we have our meeting in Provence next month?" Provence is our nickname for where Lynn lives in Silicon Valley. The acronym AAM on our calendars indicates a scheduled All About Me activity—time for a massage, run, hair color, whatever we feel like doing.

These codes are useful on many levels. Most important, they are a form of intimacy, a bonding mechanism. They make us laugh and lighten the intensity. Obviously, laughter is an important part of our AdviseHERy Board's Sisters Pledge of Allegiance.

In Between Meetings

When we started, the AdviseHERy Board was structured around scheduled meetings. However, business issues do not always follow the clock. We now communicate more frequently, often texting or e-mailing to check in or share a note-worthy experience.

When there is a big issue that can't wait until the next meeting, we have an emergency phone call or a video conference call. For example, midway through writing this book, Lynn had two fab-ulous opportunities on the table and needed to talk them through. A text to Karen and Jackie that morning resulted in a conference call a few hours later. Input and perspective in hand, Lynn made her important decision.

When life or business become overwhelming, we call a LENO (Ladies' Emergency Night Out). A

couple glasses of wine and some good food shared with each other can be just what the doctor ordered.

The bottom line is that we know we are there for each other no matter what. As we always say, "Life happens when you're building a business."

And as you'll see in the next chapter, the three of us have had our share of life in the last few years, including death, divorce, and disability.

Words of Wisdom

- Stick to the meeting structure so everyone has an opportunity to be heard and to share.

- Be open to feedback—a good idea can come from anywhere.

- When you provide feedback, make sure it comes from a place of compassion and consideration.

- Don't take anything personally; it's all intended for your own good and growth. However, if you feel picked upon, slighted, or ignored, speak up.

- If you don't agree with some input, that's okay. Sometimes it takes a few days to think about it and let it sink in.

- Conflict and push-back will occur. They are a springboard for creativity and new perspectives.

- Respect the rules of engagement (Chapter 2). For example, if one of your rules is to turn off cell phones before each meeting, hit the off button without being asked.

- If you truly have an issue that needs immediate attention, don't wait. Ask for help.

- Communication evolves over time. We had no idea that we would collect a veritable dictionary of our own words and expressions. Your style will gel over time and will not be like ours or any other group.

- Be authentic in what you say and do at AdviseHERy Board.

- Have your structure and tools in place and get going. You have a lot to talk about.

CHAPTER 5
Our Tools

When it comes to creating process, the right tools make all the difference. We have assembled our tool chest based on our individual experiences, and we have introduced each other to new platforms and gizmos. Here are our go-to choices.

SELF-ASSESSMENT

It is important that the team members understand each other's communication styles. A work-style assessment may be helpful in learning about the personalities of everyone on the team. We found it essential. There are many tools to choose from (e.g., Meyers-Briggs, DiSC). Whatever your choice, it has to be one that becomes part of the language and culture of the group. We love Lumina Spark (www. LuminaLearning.com). When you take the Lumina assessment, you learn the combination of qualities that make up your personality. You also learn where you tend to behave on the Lumina Spark model.

- Conscientious Blue: Organized. Observing. Reliable. Objective. Evidence Based.

- Empowering Green: Intimate. Collaborative. Evolving. Calming.

- Inspiring Yellow: Sociable. Spontaneous. Imaginative. Cheerful. Demonstrative.

- Commanding Red: Purposeful. Direct. Bold. Competitive. Takes Charge.

Understanding your natural strengths makes decision-making easier. By recognizing this about each other, we can see when a storm is brewing, talk about the reasons for the stress, and help each other work through it in a constructive way. When you create a common communication framework, you are able to have direct and strong conversations without the charge behind the comments. You can agree—and just as important, disagree—without being disrespectful to each other's ideas.

On the next page is a graphic of the Lumina Spark model. Take a walk around the Mandala and determine your top three and bottom three behavioral qualities.

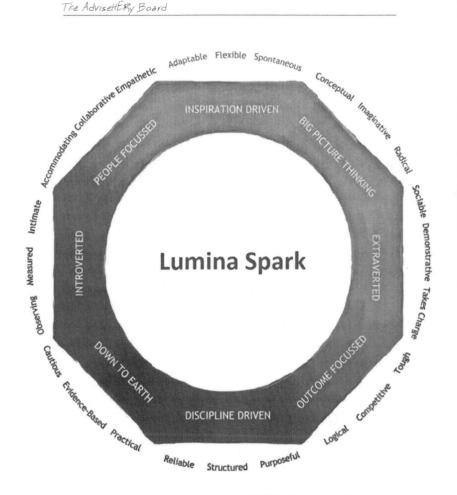

With our AdviseHERy Board, we have great similarities and wonderful differences. For instance, we are all very Take Charge and Demonstrative. You think that might get in the way sometimes?

Yup. When the inclination to take charge begins to overpower our conversation, we have learned how to tone it down in order to avoid one of us dominating the meeting and sucking out the air in the room. Being self-aware and bringing that knowledge to the forefront has been instrumental in keeping our meetings moving forward.

VIRTUAL MEETINGS

We have emphasized the importance of consistency in the meeting schedule, however meeting in person is not always an option. Virtual meetings are a great solution. There is an assortment of choices (GoToMeeting, Google Hangout, Skype, WebEx). We like video conference meetings over phone calls because video creates a more powerful human connection and forces us to stay present with each other. The AdviseHERy Board has been created as a support and kick-in-the-pants group, so you want to be prepared and be present—no multitasking!—whether the meeting is in person or virtual.

FLIP CHARTS AND MARKERS

As simple as they are, flip charts and colorful markers help us brainstorm and build on each other's ideas. We have found that we are even smarter when we are all putting our brain power into play in this visual way. We use flipcharts and markers to make lists, create action plans, and develop mind maps. If you don't have a flip chart, tape pieces of paper together and tack them to the wall. This is how we named our book! Let the ideas flow.

MIND MAPPING

All three of us are very visual, so capturing ideas in a format we could absorb was essential. We use a method called mind mapping, created by Tony Buzan, the world-renowned expert on the brain, memory, and innovation (www.tonybuzan.com). Mind mapping is a way to graphically organize ideas and concepts in a nonlinear format. It is a visual thinking tool that helps structure information, allowing you to better examine, comprehend, recall, and generate new ideas.

We have used mind mapping in many ways: to structure our AdviseHERy Board from the ground up (see our original mind map on page 50), to brainstorm about this book, and to strategize about our businesses. One of the best features of mind mapping is that a mind map can be developed anywhere and anytime. Use a lot of different colored markers when creating a mind map because that will help you remember ideas and categories. If you don't have colored markers or pens, so be it. The idea is to get your thoughts down on paper the best you can. You can add to the mind map later, cross things off, and draw pictures if you so desire.

We have a collection of our mind maps and have gone back to them many times. It has helped with the historical perspective of our AdviseHERy Board—where we have been and where we are headed.

Our Original AdviseHERy Board Mind Map

AdviseHERy Board

PURPOSE:

- KAREN
  - EXIT STRATEGY
  - SCALE THE BUSINESS
- JACKIE
  - NEW SERVICE OFFERING
  - SUCCESSION PLAN
  - Partnership
- LYNN
  - Bigger Idea
  - Multiple revenue streams
  - Build infrastructure

WHAT?

- Focus Group
- Brainstorming
- Sound Board
- Work "on" the biz NOT "IN" the biz
- structure

STRUCTURE:

- Agenda with actions from last meeting
- 30 min round robin
  - What we need
  - New Ideas generated
  - Catch up
- Each persn has 30 minutes
  - Be Prepared
  - Actions Completed
- 15-30 MINUTE CLOSE
- 1 Person Facilitates
- ONCE PER Month
  - No Longer than 6 weeks
- 2-3 Hours

RULES OF ENGAGEMENT:

- FACILITATOR:
  - REVIEWS ACTIONS
  - KEEPS MEETING MOVING
  - WATCHES Time
- BE: Kind, Truthful, Challenging, Empathetic, Smart & Present
- BRING Ideas, Resources, Wisdom
- BE: Prepared & do what you said you would do
- IT IS A "SAFE HOUSE"
- CONFIDENTIALITY RULES

GOOGLE DOCS

We wrote this book in Google Docs, which is a free, web-based application. Documents and spreadsheets can be created, edited, and stored online. Files can be accessed from any computer with an Internet connection. Google Docs allowed the three of us to access, view, and edit the same document concurrently. In this way, we did not have to send each other e-mails with attachments, wasting time trying to figure out which is the latest and greatest document. It really helped with efficiency as well. When one of us was working on one chapter, we could ask the others to review it and help us flush out ideas, add or delete content. Not that any of us are too wordy, or anything!

NOTES AND ARCHIVES

The role of the archivist is very important, and it needs to be a primary responsibility for someone in the group. We continually refer to past meetings, commitments made, ideas generated, and mind maps developed. You want one person who owns the history of your AdviseHERy Board and will be able to access what is needed on the spot. Who wouldn't want to be an archivist?

Words of Wisdom

- Be strategic. Think about the tools, techniques, and methodologies that worked in your past professional experiences and can work in this environment. There is no need to reinvent the wheel.

- Be open. Be ready to explore new ways of doing business. Be willing to move outside your comfort zone. In order to stay relevant in business and life, we have to try new things and push the boundaries. If that means learning how to use Google Docs—which drove us absolutely crazy when we first started—that's okay. The most important element here is to stay curious and be adventurous.

- Be fearless. FEAR stands for "False Expectations Appear Real." Take a chance, take a risk, feel the fear, and do it anyway. As Cheri Huber wrote in the Fear Book - Facing Fear Once and for All, "Resistance is one of the processes that mask fear, and every time we choose safety, we reinforce fear."

- Get help; it's worth it. We all need a little help from our friends (thank you, John and Paul). In addition to the AdviseHERy Board, we have all individually hired coaches or experts from time to time when needed.

- Build knowledge. Create a success library. We have ideas in the Recommended Reading section. Use ours, create your own, and send us your ideas at AdviseHERyBoard@gmail.com.

CHAPTER 6

Life Happens

Hopefully, you will make it through a few meetings before life hits you in the face. If it hasn't already, believe us, it will. There will be very good reasons and many marginally legitimate justifications to let your AdviseHERy Board commitment slip, but this is a no-excuse zone. Keep going!

We may not own the market on very good reasons and marginally legitimate justifications, but by anyone's definition, we've had some doozies. Reva, one of Karen's dear friends, died suddenly of a heart attack at age fifty-five, leaving two young children. A few months later, Jackie's beloved mom died at the lovely age of ninety-two (Hi, Rose!). Jackie's husband, Jim, suffered a mild stroke. (Was that before or after he sold his business of twenty years? We don't remember). Lynn got engaged and was planning a wedding while she and her fiancé, Jim (all three of us have—or rather, had—husbands named Jim), were in the middle of a two-year remodeling project and living temporarily in a tiny cottage with their two dogs. She also made the painful decision to put her startup on the back burner. Hurricane Sandy devastated the part of New Jersey where Karen spent her summers, and where many of her family members live. Jackie broke her left foot, and when she was out of the boot, she broke it again. Karen's nineteen-year marriage ended in the blink of an eye.

Yep, doozies.

And that's not even counting the everyday realities of life: hectic schedules, staying healthy, family obligations—we could go on forever.

It wasn't easy, but through all these heady, happy, crying-our-eyes-out times,

we kept our businesses and AdviseHERy Board going. The structure and stability of our meetings helped us stay focused and remain productive. The support and friendship we provided each other was a lifeline. And let's face it: there will always be reasons to not do something. Our ideology is to keep moving forward, even a little bit, and surround ourselves with people whose favorite word is yes.

However, don't let your AdviseHERy Board become the dreaded task. On the days that you feel you are forcing yourself to attend a meeting, remember that AdviseHERy Board is just as much about the small moments as the big ideas. Being in each other's company is sometimes just what you need to keep on keepin' on. You never know when someone will make that one comment that gets through to your muddled brain and makes a difference.

Flexibility is essential. We have rescheduled meetings many times to accommodate travel, flu, demanding clients, and other unavoidable calendar busters. We make it work one way or another. Stay true to your commitment, be open, and lean on your AB sisters. The AdviseHERy Board will not let you down.

One day, you may notice that your meetings feel stale, or that you're not getting as much out of them as you once did. If this happens, go back to Chapter 3 for meeting structure guidelines, do some soul searching, and review the original work you did to come up with the purpose and outcomes for forming your group. What can you do to keep your AdviseHERy Board fresh and a valuable asset to your business? Just do it.

Clearly, one of the main messages of this book is to make your AdviseHERy Board a priority, or else it won't work. Your business does not distinguish between this good day and this very, very bad day. Without your continual attention, your business will fail, and so will your AdviseHERy Board. And we just can't have that.

CHAPTER 7

Wrap-Up

Just get going! Call your people and set up a meeting. If you focus too long and too hard on the design of the group, you won't get to the work, or the fun. We lucked out and hit on a formula that really worked for us right from the beginning. There have been tweaks and adjustments along the way, but we basically function the same today as we did then, only better. It may take you longer to hit that magic point, and it's okay. You have begun your journey. You are not living your life or running your business by default. You are on your way. We are so excited for you because we know how powerful your very own AdviseHERy Board can be.

We're here to help. Check out our website at www.AdviseHERyBoard.com. Sign up for our e-mail list. Join our community on our Facebook page at www.facebook.com/theadviseheryboard. Tell us about your success stories and ask us your questions at AdviseHERyBoard@gmail.com.

We would love to meet you, and to speak at your next function! We're smart and fun, and we know what we're talking about.

May you stretch your goals
to meet your true potential.

May you be surrounded by people
to inspire and guide you.

May you laugh from the top
of your head to the tips of your toes.

May your ideas be ever flowing
and your profits be ever growing.

Until we meet again, long live
your AdviseHERy Board.

~~The End~~

The Beginning

RECOMMENDATIONS

SUCCESS LIBRARY

All I Really Needed to Know I Learned in Kindergarten by Robert Fulghum

Buddhist Boot Camp by Timber Hawkeye

Built to Sell: Creating a Business That Can Thrive Without You by John Warrillow

The Fear Book: Facing Fear Once and For All by Cheri Huber

Getting Things Done: The Art of Stress-Free Productivity by David Allen

Grit: The Power of Passion and Perseverance by Angela Duckworth

I Never Signed Up for This: Finding Power in Life's Broken Pieces by Darryle Pollack

Man's Search for Meaning by Viktor Frankl

Oh, The Places You'll Go by Dr. Seuss

Positive Intelligence: Why Only 20% of Teams and Individuals Achieve Their True Potential by Shirzad Chamine

Rising Strong: The Reckoning, The Rumble, The Revolution by Brene Brown

7 Habits of Highly Effective People: Powerful Lessons in Personal Change by Stephen R. Covey

Strategic Focus: The Art of Strategic Thinking by Cecilia Lynch

Thrive: The Third Metric to Redefining Success and Creating a Life of Well-Being, Wisdom, and Wonder by Arianna Huffington

The Wisdom of Teams: Creating the High-Performance Organization by Jon R. Katzenbach and Douglas K. Smith (Chapter 2)

The Year of Yes: How to Dance it Out, Stand in the Sun and Be Your Own Person by Shonda Rhimes

TOOLS

- Google Docs—We wrote our book using Google Docs. It keeps all documents up-to-date and accessible to everyone.

- Lumina Learning—Provides information on the Personality Assessment we use for communication, www.LuminaLearning.com

- Get your very own personal Lumina Spark Portrait. Contact Karen Colligan: KColligan@PeopleThink.biz

- Mind Mapping—Tony Buzan, www.tonybuzan.com/about/mind-mapping/

- Virtual Conference Tools—There are a lot on the market. Choose the one best suited for your needs.

- The Pomodoro 25-minute Timer—"The Pomodoro Technique," Stay focused and move! pomodorotechnique.com

KAREN COLLIGAN is a dyed-in-the wool Jersey girl whose "get real" approach and quick sense of humor have inspired leaders, teams, and individuals to achieve peak performance. As a corporate leader and sought-after consultant, Karen has helped transform organizations through a simple mantra: take care of your people, and they'll take care of your business. Her engaging style and vast expertise make her a popular speaker at cross-industry venues, sales meetings, and corporate conferences. Karen migrated a number of years ago from New Jersey to San Francisco, and she loves both the East and West Coast, just as long as she is near the ocean. She is an avid runner and loves music, cooking, and bringing people together for good food and lots of laughter. She does not believe that curiosity killed the cat, and her adventurous spirit keeps her bucket list growing!

Karen lives her life following the wise words of Oscar Wilde: "Be yourself. Everyone else is already taken."

LYNN FORBES has been moving full speed ahead since the day she opened her eyes. Family lore has it that when she was six weeks old, she almost wiggled off Great-Aunt Margaret's lap. She is a highly experienced editorial professional and journalist with expertise in content strategy, digital marketing, and editorial operations. Lynn has worked with many organizations, including the Hearst Corporation, Disney, Scripps Networks, Stanford and the Bay Area News Group. Writing this book has been a content dream come true.

Lynn is the proud mom of two amazing daughters and lives in California with her wonderful contractor, winemaker, guitarist husband and two goofy Corgi mutts. Her motto is "Live like you mean it."

JACKIE KLEINMAN, a native of Cincinnati, Ohio, was bitten by wanderlust at an early age. Once she got the bug, nothing was going to hold her back. Though she was encouraged to pursue a career with practical skills she could "fall back on," Jackie chose instead to set her sights on moving forward, beginning with a move to San Francisco.

After finishing her degree at the University of San Francisco, Jackie began her career in financial planning in a large corporation. Six years later, she took a leap forward and opened her own financial planning firm, KB Financial Advisors. She built it, and they came. Today she has a thriving finance and tax business catering to busy technology professionals. KB Advisors' Compound Your Potential™ approach navigates clients through complex financial decisions so they can focus on what they do best.

Jackie lives and works in San Francisco with her husband, Jim Brightman, CPA. When they are not advising clients on taxes, investments and stock options they are taking advantage of what the City by the Bay has to offer or traveling the globe in search of even more adventures. Jackie agrees with Mark Twain: "Twenty years from now you will be more disappointed by the things you didn't do than by the ones you did do."

> " Never doubt that a small group of thoughtful, committed people can change the world; indeed it is the only thing that ever has.
>
> — *Margaret Mead* — "